THE G

THE GRAND GRIMOIRE

THE RED DRAGON

Teaching the mode of summoning Lucifuge Rofocale, and obtaining one's desires.

ORIGINAL MANUSCRIPT 1750
NEW EDITION 2015
EDITED AND ILLUSTRATED BY
TARL WARWICK

THE GRAND GRIMOIRE

No part of this edition may be reproduced, copied, or distributed in any form whether digital or physical without express written consent. The original manuscript is freely available and out of copyright.

THE GRAND GRIMOIRE

FOREWORD

The *Grand Grimoire* has been known by many names. It is true that a possibly older manuscript appears to be in existence and in the possession of the Vatican, although this particular work here is the only one in public circulation which rightfully bears the title "Red Dragon."

Through these passages, the occultist is meant to be able to secure a sort of ritualistic pact with a being termed "Lucifuge" (almost certainly used in place of Lucifer.) The connection between this work and the apocryphal writings which were left out of the bible dealing with Solomon and his power over certain demonic forces is key here; and a similar phenomenon appears to have led to the penning of the *Lesser Keys*. There are other grimoires as well from around the same time period, as well as after, such as the *Black Pullet* with similar mysterious dates and manners of manufacture, but the Grand Grimoire is probably the best known of them with the exception of the oft-reprinted Lesser Keys.

The work has been conflated with at least three other grimoires; none of them are the actual red dragon, and only this work, with its Lucifuge references, is authentic; it has often been reprinted with passages or books from other sources added on, likely due to its relatively short length; these include the original *Key of Solomon* and the latter *Ars Notoria* amongst others. Often, these inclusions do serve a purpose however, since there are similarities in the rites and workings.

The work essentially contains three sections; the first being an extremely lengthy ritual designed to obtain communication with the demon in question, after which there is an extensive section in Latin, and subsequently a large number of short spells and incantations for various purposes, such as traveling at great speed among other things of a somewhat unbelievable nature.

Oddly, unlike other texts from this period, there appears to be little if any steganographic purpose behind this work; in many cases we see philosophical allusions hidden in the text or the invocations themselves which would be unnoticed by untrained laypeople and may have been meant to impart a different meaning altogether from the literal, to those who are already aware of who was authoring the work and the types of clues they would be likely to include. This saved, likely, many people from the gallows at the time.

We do find at least a few humorous swipes at going European culture, especially in Lucifer's articles.

We may regard the *Grand Grimoire* as somewhat unique among grimoires from its time period; for this lack of symbolism appears to render it more of a folk treatise, perhaps conglomerated from multiple incantations and spells collected over some period of time, perhaps by a heretical order or perhaps by an actual sorcerer seeking to expand their repertoire.

Regardless of its authorship the work has been studied in detail by most serious black magicians; the rites herein are at the very least interesting and exciting, if not necessarily "real." Those who have ever worked such incantations know there is something there though; maybe a secret that we have simply lost in time because those privy to it predeceased us by 500 years.

The concept behind this work at its root depends upon which specific version is used; it appears that the latter (Italian) edition has had certain folk rites and beliefs tacked onto it. I have preserved them here for two reasons. Firstly, the material dates to nearly the same time period as the original manuscript anyways, and secondly the rites specifically mentioned may indeed, if this is a steganographic work revolving around enlightenment philosophy masquerading as magick, be from the same general group of intellectuals, perhaps included indeed with their blessing. Like the infamous Grimorium Verum (which I have also edited and released) some versions also include material from Thelema, which comes not from the enlightenment but rather the early modern period and is useless in the context of such a grimoire. I am unsure as to why such groups persist at their revisionism.

THE GRAND GRIMOIRE

As with many other works from this and earlier periods, some strange capitalization occurs whenever some purported power of Jehovah is mentioned, as well as, (and herein is what makes this text a bit of a philosophical outlier) when demonic forces are mentioned or invoked. Even the practice of signing ones' name in blood, as in this text, as part of a "demonic" pact, is relatively uncommon in actual grimoires, and mostly they revolve around celestial movements and simple invocations, especially from Kabbalistic lore; oddly, this work specifically credits the Kabbalists with some of its content while including invocations and practices which are more christianized in form, or else folkish and therefore perhaps older and pagan, specifically in the European tradition.

Even the images included with the work appear to tell a sort of steganographic story; here we see the figure of Astaroth, lord (here) of the Americas. How strange that the face shown here appears to depict (crudely) one of Native American origin.

With great reverence, thus, now you may delve at your leisure into the pages of the Grand Grimoire.

BOOK I

SECTION I

This Book is so rare and sought after in our country it has been called, by our Rabbis, the true Great Work. They were the ones who left us this precious original that many charlatans uselessly wanted to counterfeit, attempting to imitate the truth that they never found, in order to swindle ingenuous individuals who have faith in initial encounters without seeking their true Source.

This manuscript has been copied from various writings of the great King Solomon. This great king spent all of his days in the most difficult search and in the most obscure and unexpected secrets. In the end he succeeded in all of his endeavors and he reached his goal of penetrating the most profound dwelling of the spirits, whom he obliged to obey him by the power of his talisman, the clavicle, since who else but this powerful genius would have dared bring to light the thundering words that he made use of to constrain the rebel spirits to his will, having penetrated up to the celestial beings to learn more thoroughly the secrets and the powerful words that have the force of a terrible and respected God?

This great King discovered the secrets of which the great Divinity made use, and then enabled us to understand the influence of the stars, the constellation of the planets. To prepare the fulminating rod, with it's effects which make the spirits tremble and of which God made use of to arm the angel who expelled Adam and Eve from the Garden of Eden; with which God struck down the Rebel Angels, precipitating their pride into the most horrendous abyss. With the power of this rod clouds are formed, hurricanes are dispersed and one can make them fall on the part of the earth that one desires.

THE GRAND GRIMOIRE

SECTION II

Weak men and mortals! Tremble at your temerity when you blindly think that you possess such a profound science. You are taking your spirit beyond its spheres. Learn from me that before undertaking this work it is necessary to be steadfast, constant and most careful to observe exactly, point by point, everything that I will tell you without which everything would rebound to your disadvantage, confusion and total loss. If, to the contrary, you perform exactly that which I tell you, you will leave behind your baseness and indigence and you will have full success in all of your enterprises.

Arm yourselves then with trepidation, prudence and virtuosity in order to succeed at this great and immense task, at which I have spent 67 years working day and night. To succeed at this great goal it is necessary to do exactly that which I will hereby indicate.

-Solomon

THE GRAND GRIMOIRE

PRINCIPIO

You will pass a quarter of a month abstaining from the company of the opposite sex, so as to not fall into impurity.

Begin the quarter of a month by promising to the great Adonay, who is the leader of all of the spirits, to have two meals a day every 24 hours of the above-mentioned quarter month, during which you will eat at midday and midnight, or at seven in the morning and seven in the evening, reciting the following prayer before dining for this entire period.

The manner in which one can make any sort of spirit appear, reciting the great invocation that you will find in this book. So also, the true method of preparation.

PRAYER

"I implore you, oh great and powerful ADONAY, head of all spirits. I implore you O ELOHIM I implore you O JEHOVA, oh great King ADONAY, condescend to be favorable. So it shall be. Amen."

Then eat your meals, and don't undress, and sleep as little as possible for the prescribed quarter of a month, continually thinking of your undertaking and putting all of your faith and hope in the infinite good of the Great Adonay.

The second day of this period, you will buy a bloodstone called Ematille from the druggist and you will always carry it with you and it will preserve you from all fears and worries since the spirit that you intend to bring into your servitude will do all that he can to dissuade you from your undertaking, believing with these means to liberate himself and thereby break the twines of the net that you begin to fasten around him. This project must be undertaken only by one other person, including the Karcist, (the one who must speak to the spirit), keeping in his hand the fulminating wand.

THE GRAND GRIMOIRE

It is essential to choose a solitary location for this operation, which is far from any uproar, so that the operator is not interrupted. Following this, you will buy a young virgin kid (goat), that on the third day of the quarter you will adorn with a garland of Verbena (or, the sacred herb) which you will attach to his head with a green ribbon. Then you will transport it to the place that has been chosen for your operation; your right arm will be bare to the shoulder, armed with a blade of pure steel, a fire of white wood will be lit, you will say the following words with hope and resolve.

FIRST OFFERING

"I offer you this victim, O great ADONAY, ELOHIM, ARIEL and JEHOVA, and this in the honor, glory and power of your superior and to all if the spirits, be so kind, O great ADONAY, as to appreciate it. Amen."

Following this you will skin the kid and take its skin, putting the rest of it in the fire until it is reduced to ashes, which you will gather and throw to the rising sun pronouncing the following words:

"It is for the honor, glory and power of your name, O ADONAY, ELOHIM, ARIEL and JEHOVA, that I shed the blood of this victim. Deign yourself to accept these ashes, O great ADONAY."

While the sacrifice burns, rejoice in the honor and glory of the great ADONAY, ELOHIM, ARIEL and JEHOVA taking care to conserve the kids skin to make the round, or the grand Kabbalistic circle in which you will stay the day of the great undertaking.

THE GRAND GRIMOIRE

SECTION III

Containing the true composition of the mysterious or fulminating wand, as it is depicted here:

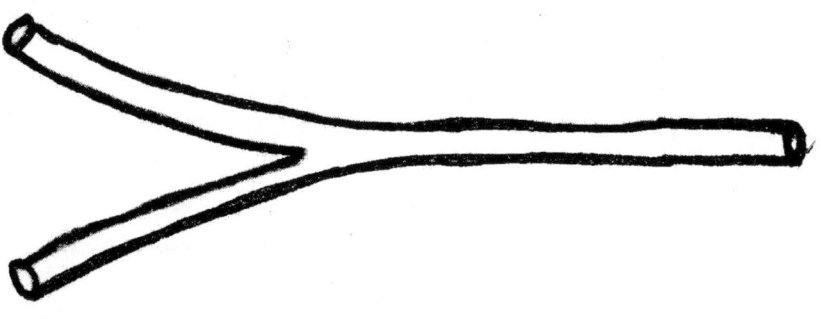

On the eve of the great undertaking you will search for a rod or wand of wild hazel tree that has not yet born fruit, at the highest point of the sought-after branch there should be a second little branch in the form of a fork with two ends; its length should be nineteen and a half inches.

After having found a branch of this shape, only look at it but abstain from touching it, waiting for the following day, a day destined for action, in which you will go and cut it precisely at sunrise, and denude it of its leaves and small twigs, if there are any of these, and with the same blade that was used to skin the sacrifice, which will still be tainted with its blood; you will cut it when the sun starts to break forth on this hemisphere, pronouncing the following words:

"I beseech you, O great ADONAY, ELOHIM, ARIEL and JEHOVA to be favorable and to give this rod that I am cutting the strength of Jacob and the virtue of Moses and that of the great Joshua; and I beseech you, O great ADONAY, ELOHIM, ARIEL and JEHOVA to enclose in this rod all the power of Samson, the righteous rage of

THE GRAND GRIMOIRE

Emmanuel and the Thunderbolt of ZARIATNATMICK who will avenge man's affronts on the day of Judgment."

After having pronounced these great and terrible words, always keeping your eyes turned toward the rising sun, cut the branch and take it to your room, then take a piece of wood that is of the same thickness as the two ends of the rod and take it to a Smith to cap the two ends of the fork with the steel blade that was used to skin the sacrifice, ensuring that the two blades are sharp and when they are fitted to the two pieces of wood, take them home, putting the two irons on the true rod yourself, then take a lodestone, heat it in the fire to magnetize the points of the rod pronouncing the following words:

"By the power of the great ADONAY, ELOHIM, ARIEL and JEHOVA, I beseech you to unite all of the materials that I desire by the power of the great ADONAY, ELOHIM, ARIEL and JEHOVA I command you by the incorruptibility of water and fire, to separate all of the materials as they were separated the day of the creation of the world. Amen."

Following this I assure you (in the honor of the great ADONAY) being certain that you possess the greatest Treasure of the Light. The following evening take your rod, the kid skin, the Bloodstone, the two garlands of Verbena, then also, the two candle holders and two pounds of virgin wax that has been blessed; take also the lodestone and two smooth flint-stones to light the fire also half a bottle of Spirit of Water and a portion of blessed incense mixed with some camphor and four nails that were used in the coffin of a child who has recently died. Then take yourself to the place where you have to do the Great Work, doing exactly the following, executing point-by-point the great Kabbalistic Circle in the manner indicated:

THE GRAND GRIMOIRE

SECTION IV

Containing the true method to make the great Kabbalistic circle.

Start by forming a circle with the kid skin that you will nail down with the four nails, then with the Bloodstone you will make a triangle inside of the circle, starting from the direction of the rising sun; make also with the bloodstone the four letters that are written outside of the circle. So also the saintly name of Jesus in this manner: JHS between two crosses so that the spirits can't harm you from behind.

Following this, the Karcist (who is the operator) will let his associates into the Triangle and he will also enter without letting himself become frightened by any noise that he could hear, putting the two candle holders with the two garlands of Verbena to the right and to the left of the internal triangle. That done, light the two candles and put a new vase in front of you, that is, in front of the Karcist, filled with the ash of the willow wood that you have burned earlier that same day.

The Karcist will light it and pouring in a part of the Spirit of Water and part of the incense and camphor, and conserving the remaining part to maintain a continuous flame that will suffice for the entire operation.

Having done everything exactly as has been described here you will pronounce the following words:

"I present you, O great ADONAY, this incense as the most pure, at the same time I present you with these ashes which come from the lightest wood. I offer you them, O great ADONAY, ELOHIM, ARIEL and JEHOVA, with all my heart and spirit. Condescend, O great ADONAY, to accept them. Amen."

Pay attention not to have any impure metal on your person but only some gold or silver coins folded in a piece of paper to throw at the spirit so that he cannot harm you when he presents himself to you before the circle and while he takes the coin you will begin the following prayer, arming yourself with courage, strength and prudence.

Be careful that only the Karcist speaks; the others must remain silent, even if the spirit interrogates or threatens them.

First Oration:

"O great living God, the only and same person, the Father, the Son, and the Holy Ghost, I adore you with the most profound respect and I submit myself to your saintly and worthy custody with full faith. I sincerely believe that you are my creator, my benefactor and my support and master; I declare to you that I have no other wish but that of belonging to you for eternity. So it shall be. Amen."

Second Oration:

"O great living God, who created man to be happy in this life and who created everything for our needs, and who said that everything shall be dependent on man; be favorable and do not permit that the rebel spirits possess the treasures that were formed by your hands for earthly needs. Give me, O great God, the faculty to possess them by the powerful and terrible words of the Clavicle: ADONAY, ELOHIM, ARIEL, JEHOVA, TAGLA, MATHON. Be favorable. So shall it be."

Be careful to maintain your flame with the spirits of the wine, incense and camphor and then make the following offering.

"I offer you this incense as the purest that I could find, O great ADONAY, ELOHIM, ARIEL and JEHOVA design to accept it. O great ADONAY use your power to be favorable and enable me to succeed in this great undertaking. So it shall be. Amen."

First Invocation to Emperor Lucifer:

"Emperor Lucifer, prince and master of the rebel spirits, I implore you to abandon your dwelling, in whatever part of the world you should be, to come and speak to me. I command and entreat you by the authority

of the great living God, the Father, the Son and the Holy Spirit, to come noiselessly and without giving off any offensive scents, to respond in a clear and intelligible voice, point by point, to all that I shall ask you, failing which, thou shalt be most surely compelled to obedience by the power of the divine ADONAY, ELOHIM, ARIEL, JEHOVA, TAGLA, MATHON, and by the whole hierarchy of superior spirits, who shall constrain you against your will."

Second Invocation to Emperor Lucifer:

"I command and entreat you Emperor Lucifer, by the authority of the great living God, by the power of EMMANUEL his Son, your only master and mine, and by virtue of his precious blood which he spilled to liberate man from his chains, I order you to abandon your dwelling in whatever part of the world you should be, swearing to you that I will not give you a moment of rest, but that you come to speak to me immediately with an intelligent voice or, if you cannot come in person, send me your messenger Astaroth in human guise noiselessly and without foul scents otherwise I will strike you and your entire kind with the blasting rod as far as the bottom of the abysses and it will be with the power of these great words of the Clavicle, by ADONAY, ELOHIM, ARIEL, JEHOVA, TAGLA, MATHON, ALMOZIN, ARIOS, PITHONIA, MAGOTS, SYLPHAE, TABOTS, SALAMANDRAE, GNOMUS, TERRAE, CELLIS, GODIUS, AQUA; immediately."

Warning:

Prior to the reading of the third invocation, if the spirit doesn't appear, read the Clavicle as follows, and strike all of the spirits, putting the two ends of the fork of your rod in the fire. At this point do not be frightened by the horrible cries that you will hear because all of the spirits will appear. Before reading the Clavicle, while the noise continues, read again the third invocation.

Third Invocation to Emperor Lucifer:

"I command you, Emperor Lucifer, by the great living God, his

THE GRAND GRIMOIRE

dear son and the Holy Ghost and by the power of the great ADONAY, ELOHIM, ARIEL AND JEHOVA, to appear now or send me your ASTAROTH. I command you to abandon your dwelling in whatever part of the world it should be, declaring to you that if you do not appear immediately, I will strike you and all of your cohorts again with the blasting rod of the great ADONAY, ELOHIM, ARIEL AND JEHOVA."

If the spirit still has not appeared put the two ends of your rod in the fire and read the following words of Solomon's Clavicle.

Grand Invocation of the Great Kabbala:

"I supplicate you, O Spirit! by the power of the grand ADONAY, to appear instantly, and by ELOHIM, by ARIEL, by JEHOVA, by AGLA, TAGLA, MATHON, OARIOS, ALMOAZIN, ARIOS, MEMBROT, VARIOS, PITHONA, MAJODS, SULPHAE, GABOTS, SALAMANDRAE, TABOTS, GINGUA, JANNA, ETITNAMUS, ZARIATNATMIX, etc.. A C E C A C J C A C T C M C O C A C A C M C V C P C M C S C C C S C J C C C G C A C J C F C Z C etc.."

After having twice repeated these great and powerful words you can be sure that the spirit will appear in the following manner.

The Apparition of the Spirit:

Here I am, what will you ask of me? Why do you torment my peace? Desist from striking me again with that terrible rod."
-Lucifuge Rofocale

Query to the Spirit:

"Had you appeared when I called you, I would not have struck you: consider that if you do not confer upon me that which I ask, I will eternally torment you."
-Solomon

THE GRAND GRIMOIRE

Response of the Spirit:

"Do not bother or disturb me further. Tell me immediately what you want."
    -Lucifuge Rofocale

Query to the Spirit:

"I command you to come and speak to me twice daily during the night, or to those who have the book which you will approve and sign. I will leave it to you to choose which times are most convenient to you, if you do not want to approve the following times hereby indicated, that is:

    On Monday at nine o'clock and at midnight.
    On Tuesday at ten o'clock and at one in the morning.
    On Wednesday at eleven o'clock and at two in the morning.
    On Thursday at eight and ten o'clock.
    On Friday at seven in the evening and at midnight.
    On Saturday at nine in the evening and at eleven at night.

Moreover, I command you to give me the nearest treasure and I promise you as reward the first piece of gold or silver which I touch with my hands on the first day of every month. Here is what I ask of you."
    -Solomon

Response of the Spirit:

"I cannot grant that which you ask of me, if not on this, nor on any others, unless you give yourself over to me in fifty years, to do with thy body and soul as I please.
    -Lucifuge Rofocale

THE GRAND GRIMOIRE

Query to the Spirit:

"I am going to strike you and all of your cohorts by the power of the great ADONAY if you do not immediately grant to me that which I ask of you."

-Solomon

Warning:

Put the two ends of the blasting rod in the fire again; rereading the great invocation of the Clavicle, until the spirit submits to your wishes.

Response and Covenant with the Spirit:

"Do not strike me anymore! I promise to do everything that you want. Two hours at night-time every day of the week, that is:

On Monday at ten o'clock and at midnight.
On Tuesday at eleven o'clock and at one in the morning.
On Wednesday at midnight and at two in the morning.
On Thursday at eight and eleven o'clock.
On Friday at nine in the evening and at midnight.
On Saturday at ten o'clock in the evening and at one in the morning.

I also approve your book and I give my signature in parchment which I will attach to this book so that you can use it for your needs; I also submit myself to appear before you whenever I am called and when you open the book and are purified and have the terrible blasting rod and have prepared the great Kabbalistic circle and pronouncing the name Rofocale. I promise to appear and treat you, and those who have this book which will bear my signature, considerately and in a friendly manner as long as you shall call me to order as soon as have need of me. I shall also induce myself to give you the treasure for which you have asked, provided that you keep the secret forever; that you shall be charitable towards the poor and that you give me a gold or silver coin all the first days of every month.

If you neglect to do this things you shall be mine forever."

-Lucifuge Rofocale, Approved.

The signature:

Response to the Spirit:

"I will adhere to your demand."
-Solomon

Orders of the Spirit:

"Follow me and you will come to identify the treasure."

Then the Karcist, armed with the blasting rod and the bloodstone, will leave the circle at that point where the door of mighty ADONAY is figured, towards the place where the treasure is located, and will follow the spirit; the others shall not move from there place in the circle and shall remain there without any fear, despite the noise that they will hear and any vision that they see.

The spirit will then take the Karcist to the entrance of the treasure and it might be that the Karcist will see something like a big dog with a collar that shines like the Sun that will block the entrance; this is the gnome that you will drive away from you by presenting the forked part of the rod, then he will walk towards the treasure. You will follow him and having arrived at the treasure, you will be surprised to see the person who originally hid it, who will want to throw himself over it however he will not be able to approach it. It is necessary to be armed with a sheet of virgin parchment on which you will have written the great conjuration of the Clavicle which you will throw over the treasure.

At the same time, take a coin as a token of gratitude, and throwing first one of yours that you have bitten and withdrawing backwards, that is, with your shoulders back, taking with you all of the coins that you can from the treasure. The rest can not disappear considering the precautions that have been taken. Be careful not to turn back despite any noise you might hear since at the time it will seem to you that all of the mountains of the world are falling on your head.

It is necessary to arm yourself with intrepidity and not to become frightened, but to remain resolute whilst the spirit conducts you back to the entrance of the circle. The Karcist will begin to read the returning of the spirit, as follows.

Entreating and Returning of the Spirit:

"Oh Prince Lucifer, I am satisfied with you at the present; I leave you in peace and I will permit you to retire to wherever you please, without making any noise or leaving bad odors; think of your promise, since if you fail for even a moment to fulfill your duties you can be certain that I will strike you eternally with the fulminating rod of the great ADONAY, ELOHIM, ARIEL and JEHOVA. Amen."

Rendering Thanks:

"Oh great God, you who have created all things for the service and utility of man, we render you humble thanks for all of your generosity which has overwhelmed tonight and for all your precious favors and for that which you have granted us, fulfilling all of our desires. At present, O great God, we have come to know the extent of the power of your great promises taken when you said "seek and you shall find", "knock and the door shall be opened", since you have recommended that we help the poor; we promise by the great ADONAY, ELOHIM, ARIEL and JEHOVA to be charitable and to spread over them the rays of the Sun of which these four powerful divinities have come to cover us. So it shall be. Amen."

CENTUM REGNUM

Conjuring Lucifer:

"LUCIFER, OUIA, KAMERON, ALISCOT, MANDESUMINI, POEMI, ORIEL, MAGREUSE, PARINOSCON, ESTIO, DUMOGON, DIVORCON, CASMIEL, HUGRAS, FABIEL, VONTON, ULI, SODIERNO, PETAN! Come LUCIFER. Amen."

The Promise of the Spirit:

First Article:

I, Lucifer, am the extremely powerful Emperor, supreme and independent, free and absolute ruler of the subterranean kingdom, despotic lord over all my jurisdiction. I, the formidable, terrible, most noble, rule everything in the most regular fashion, moving and governing the fortunes and misfortunes of my subjects with absolute power, wise and sagacious, endowed with the most sublime and luminous character, am the dominator of Europe and of all misfortunes in general.

Second Article:

I promise and swear, in the name of the God of the living, obedience, promptitude, and submission to the owner of this book; signed and sworn, in the name of the undersigned and of my aforementioned subjects, and by the virtue of the oath and signature I swear to adhere to all that will please the owner of this book.

Third Article:

Additionally, as for one of my own subjects that reading my summons from the first article may cause them to appear at once in the guise of a handsome young man with a pleasing appearance without making any uproar or noise or anything else that might cause my master to be offended or frightened, to respond truthfully and clearly, without duplicity, to his interrogations and to fulfill that which is commanded of me, with complete loyalty and sincerely, without spreading scents or any other magical invocations, actions or ceremonies but rather to appear instantaneously ready to execute your commands.

Fourth Article:

Without in these occasions ever, ever, ever damaging the countryside or anything else that springs from the earth. I will accomplish my service and leave at once without causing any commotion.

Fifth Article:

Additionally, I promise and swear to the aforesaid: servitude of all my subjects to the owner of this book without differentiation in rank, dignity or any other division but any time, in any weather, season, year, month, week, day, hour or quarter, that at the moment my invocation is read to provide any of my subjects to appear in the form of a handsome young man to the service of the owner of this book and not to leave unless I or my subjects given license with the simple formula, either from myself or from others.

Sixth Article:

Moreover, I promise and swear my subjects in the name of God and of other mysterious dispositions will practice secrecy and invincible loyalty without ever failing to fulfill my oath and promises.

Seventh Article:

Also I promise and swear on behalf of all my subjects to protect and defend the owner of this book from all misfortunes, dangers and other natural and accidental occurrences, and for whatever he might want when I am called to assist him with anything he might need, although it is not noted in this book.

Method of Dismissal:

"I leave you in peace and I will permit you to retire to wherever you please, to return immediately with my invocation. In the name of the Father, The Son and the Holy Spirit. Amen."

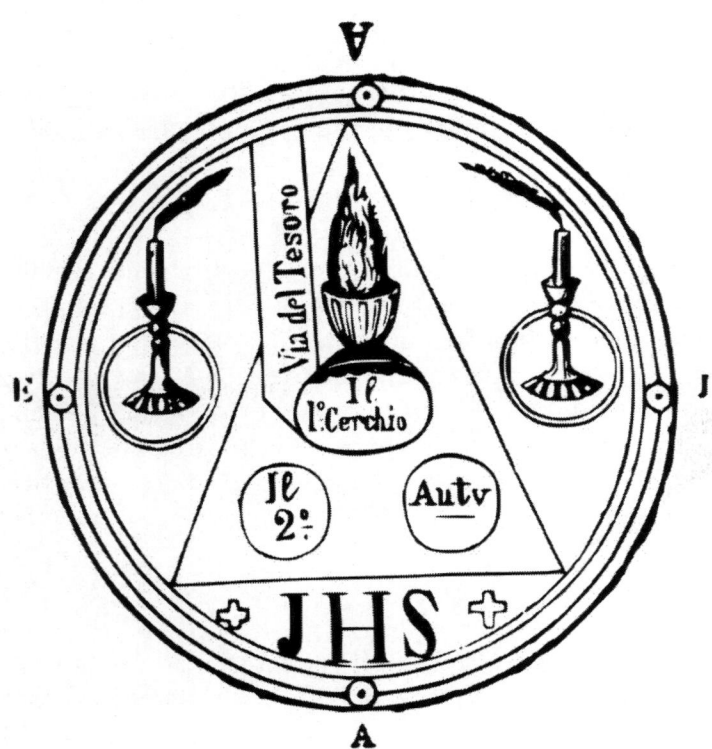

THE SECOND BOOK

The Second Book containing the Sanctum Regnum of the Clavicle or the true manner of making pacts, with the names and powers and talents of all of the great superior Spirits and also the manner of making them appear by the power of the great invocations of the chapter of the pacts of the Clavicle that forces them to obey in whatever operation one wishes to execute.

Following other Magick Secrets:

The true manner of making pacts with any spirit without them being able to do you any harm. The true Sanctum Regnum of the great Clavicle otherwise referred to as Pacta Conventa Daemoniorum which has already been talked about for a long while, is a necessary thing for the understanding of those who want to force the spirits and who do not have the capacity to prepare the blasting rod or the Kabbalistic circle that were discussed in the preceding book.

The individuals cannot arrive at their goal of forcing any spirit to appear if they don't do exactly that which I will hereby describe, concerning the manner of making pacts with any spirit, whether it is for gaining treasures or for the enjoyment of some earthly pleasure, or whatever favor one would desire or in order to discover the most hidden secrets of all of the courts and cabinets of the world; be it to reveal the most impenetrable thoughts to make or constrain a spirit to work at nighttime at whatever task; to make it hail or storm wherever it pleases you and you see fit; to render yourself invisible; to have yourself transported to any part of the earth; to open all of the keyholes and see everything that occurs in the houses of others; so also to gain understanding of necromancy or to gain glory, to know all of the qualities and virtues of all the minerals, vegetables and all of the animals, pure and impure, and to do many very surprising things.

THE GRAND GRIMOIRE

There is no man who does not become astonished at the discovery that in making a pact with a spirit one can unveil nature's greatest secrets that have remained hidden from the eyes of all men and by means of the great King Solomon's Clavicle the true manner of making pacts has been discovered and that he himself made use of it to acquire many riches and to enjoy many women and to know the most impenetrable secrets of nature which one can do any sort of good deed while avoiding any kind of evil.

Finally, at least we will begin by listing the names of the principle spirits along with their respective strengths and powers; following which we will explain the pacta daemoniorum, which contains the manner of making pacts with any spirits, with the names of the three principle spirits.

The Names and Offices of the Spirits:

Lucifer, Emperor
Belzebuth, Prince
Astaroth, Grand Duke

Then come the superior spirits who are beneath the three above mentioned, that is:

Lucifuge, Prime Minister
Satanachia, Great General
Agliarept, General
Fleurèty, Lieutenant General
Sargatanas, Brigadier
Nebiros, Camp Marshal

The first seven superior spirits that I will name direct their power over all of the internal powers and have at their service 18 other spirits that are beneath them, that is:

    1. Bael
    2. Agares
    3. Marbas

THE GRAND GRIMOIRE

4. Pruslas
5. Aamon
6. Barbatos
7. Buer
8. Gusoyn
9. Botis
10. Bathim
11. Hursan
12. Eligor
13. Loray
14. Valefor
15. Farai
16. Ayperos
17. Naberus
18. Glosialabolas

After having indicated to you the above names of the 18 spirits who are inferior to the first six already mentioned, it is necessary to understand the following, that is:

Lucifuge commands the first three who are called Bael, Agares and Marbas.

Satanachia over Pruslas, Aamon and Barbatos.

Agliarept over Buer, Cusgyn and Betis.

Fleurèty over Bathim, Hursan and Eligor.

Sargatanas over Loray, Valefar and Farai.

Nebiros over Ayperos, Naberus and Glosialabolas.

Although there are millions of spirits that are all inferior to those above, it would be useless to describe them because they are employed by the superior ones. To work in their place all of these inferior spirits are employed as if they were workers of slaves.

Now then, in making a pact with one of the first principle spirits, of which you will have need, it won't matter which spirit serves you, nonetheless always ask for the one with which you have made the pact, whether it is one of the three principle ones, or one of their subjects which serve you.

LUCIFER

LUCIFUGE

BELZEBUTH

ASTAROTH

Now you come to know the power, science, art and talents at all of the subject spirits, so that he who you would like to make a pact can find in each one of the six superior spirits the power that he will need.

The first is the great Lucifuge Rofocale, the infernal Prime Minister who possesses the power that Lucifer gave him over all worldly riches and treasures. He has beneath him Bael, Agares and Marbas along with thousands of other demons or spirits who are his subordinates.

The second is the great Satanacha, the Great General who has the power to make all young or old. Women submit to him; he commands a strong legion of spirits and has beneath him Pruslas, Aamon and Barbatos. Agaliarept, General, has the power to uncover the most well hidden secrets of all of the courts and cabinets of the world and reveals the greatest mysteries; he commands the second legion of spirits and has Guer, Gusoyn and Boris etc.. under his command.

Fleurèty, Lieutenant General, has the power has the power to do whatever thing one could want at night-time. He makes hail fall wherever he deigns and commands a considerably body of spirits and has Bathim, Hursan and Eligor etc.. beneath him.

Sargatanas, Brigadier, has the power to render one invisible and to transport you anywhere, to open all of the keyholes and to let you see what is going on in other houses and to teach you Necromancy. He commands other brigades of spirits and has beneath him Loray, Valefar and Farai, etc..

Naberus, Field Marshal, or Inspector General, has the power to do evil to whomever he pleases and enables one to find the Hand of Glory and teaches the qualities of minerals, vegetables and of all of the animals, pure and impure, possesses the art of foretelling the future, being one of the best Necromancers of all of the Infernal Spirits. He can go anywhere and inspects all of the Infernal militias and has beneath him- Ayperos, Naberus and Glosialobolas, etc..

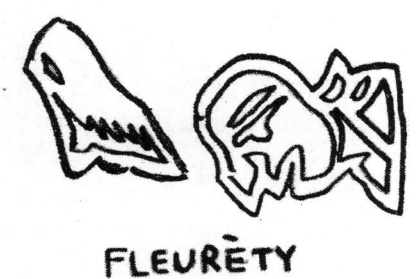

FLEURÈTY

AGLIAREPT

NEBIROS

SARGATANAS

SATANACHIA

Warning:

When you want to make your pact with one of the principal spirits that I have named, begin the day before the eve of the pact cutting a branch of wild hazel that has never bloomed with a new blade that has never been used, in the same manner that I have described in the first book, precisely at the moment that the sun appears on the horizon.

Then procure a bloodstone and two candles that have been blessed and choose a place that nobody can disturb you for the operation.

You can make a pact in a room that is far from turmoil or in some hamlet of an old, ruined castle so that the spirit has the power to transport the treasure where he pleases.

Having returned to the opportune place, draw a triangle with the bloodstone and you only need to do this operation the first time the pact is made.

THE GRAND GRIMOIRE

Then put the two blessed candles on the sides of the triangle, as is described in the triangle of the pacts, making the saintly name of Jesus behind, so that the spirits can not do you any harm.

Following this, go to the center of the triangle with the mysterious rod and the great invocation of the spirit, the Clavicle, the petition, the pact that you in mind to make with the spirit, and the sending back of the spirit as will hereby be explained. If what has been explained up to this point is executed with exactitude then start to recite the following invocation with hope and steadfast firmness:

Great Invocation to Summon the Spirit with whom one wishes to the pact excerpted from The Great Clavicle:

"Emperor LUCIFER, master of all the rebel spirits, I ask you to be favorable in my summons of your Great Minister LUCIFUGE ROFOCALE, since I wish to make a pact with him. I also request that you, Prince BELZEBUTH, protect me in my undertaking; O Come ASTAROTH BE propitious and ensure that the great LUCIFUGE appears to me tonight in human guise and without emitting foul odors and he grant me as per the pact that I will present to him, all of the riches which I require. O great LUCIFUGE, I request that you abandon your dwelling, in whatever part of the world it should be, to come and speak with me. Otherwise, I will force you by the power of the great living God and his dear Son and the Holy Spirit: obey now, or I will eternally torment you by the authority of the powerful words of Solomon's great Clavicle of which he made use to oblige the rebel Spirits to receive his pact; therefore, appear as quickly as possible or I will continually torment you by the authority of the powerful words of the Clavicle:

Aglon, Tetragram, vaycheon stimulamaton ezphares Tetragrammaton, olyaramirion esytion existion eryona onera orasim mozm messias soter Emanuel Sabaoth ADONAY, te adoro et te invoco. Amen."

You can be certain that before having finished reading the above-mentioned powerful words the spirit will appear and will tell you the following.

Apparition of the Spirit:

"Here I am. What would you ask of me? Why do you torment my rest? Answer me!"
-Lucifuge Rofocale

Request to the Spirit:

"I may ask you to make a pact with me so that you make me rich as soon as possible, otherwise I will torment you by the powerful words of the Clavicle."
-Karcist

Response of the Spirit:

"I can not grant your request except on the condition that you give yourself to me for the next 20 years so that I can use your body and soul as I see fit."
-Lucifuge Rofocale

Then you will throw him your pact, which must be in your hand writing on a sheet of virgin parchment, which will consist of these few words, with your signature written in your blood. Here is the pact:

"I promise to repay the great Lucifuge in 20 years for all of the treasures that he will give me. On my honor I sign this in good faith."

Your signature here must be signed in blood.

Response of the Spirit:

"I can not grant your request."
-Lucifuge Rofocale

THE GRAND GRIMOIRE

Second Appearance of the Spirit:

Then, in order to force the spirit to obey you, re-read the great Invocation of the terrible words of the Clavicle, until the spirit appears and tells you the following:

"Why do you torment me more and more? If you leave me in peace, I will give you the nearest treasure on the condition that you consecrate a coin to me all of the Mondays of every month and that you will call me one day every week, from ten o'clock in the evening until 2 two in the morning. Take your pact which I have signed; and if you do not maintain your word you will be mine in 20 years."
-Lucifuge Rofocale

Response to the Spirit:
"I adhere to your demands, on the condition that you enable me to have the nearest treasure and that I can take it with me right away."
-Karcist

Response of the Spirit:
"Follow me and take the treasure that I am going to show you."
-Lucifuge Rofocale

Then follow the spirit on the path to the treasure that will be indicated (at the triangle) without taking fright and throw the signed pact over the treasure and touching it with the rod take as much of it as you can. Then return inside the triangle, making certain to walk backwards, where you will deposit your treasure in front of yourself, dismissing the spirit as follows:

The Conjuring and Dismissal of the Spirit with whom the pact is made:

"O great LUCIFUGE, I am satisfied with you at present; I will leave you to peace and permit you to retire to wherever you wish without making any noise or leaving any bad odors. Think then, about your duty regarding my pact; since, if the one instant you shirk your obligation, you can be sure that I will torment you eternally with the great and powerful words of the great Clavicle of the great King Solomon with which he forced all of the rebel spirits to obey him."

Prayer to the Omnipotent in Thanksgiving:

"Omnipotent God, heavenly father, who created all things for the service and use of man, I humbly thank you, that in your great goodness and that you have permitted that I could make a pact with a spirit that is a rebel of your authority and subdue it to obey me in fulfilling all of my needs. I thank you, O omnipotent God, for the good that you have done me tonight to have shown myself to be worthy to have granted to me, miserable creature, your precious favors and to present, great God, now that I have come to know the force and power of your great promises, when you said: "seek and you shall find", "knock and the door shall be opened" as you have recommended to raise the poor, condescend O great God to inspire me to true sentiment of charity so that I can spread with this Great Work a great portion of the possessions your great divinity permitted that I could receive. Let it be, O great God, that I can enjoy these great riches that I possess, with tranquility and do not permit any rebel spirit to harm my enjoyment of these precious treasures over which you permit me to own.

Inspire in me, O great God, the necessary sentiment to unbind me from the grips of the devil and all maleficent spirits. I trust, O great God, in the Father, the Son, and the Holy Spirit and in your saintly protection. Amen."

Oration to Protect Oneself from Evil Spirits:

"O omnipotent Father, O Mother, the most tender of all mothers, O admirable example of the sentiments, O Son, O flower of all sons, soul, spirit, harmony and number of all orders, preserve us, protect us, guide us and be propitious. Amen."

CITATIO PRAEDICTORUM SPIRITUM

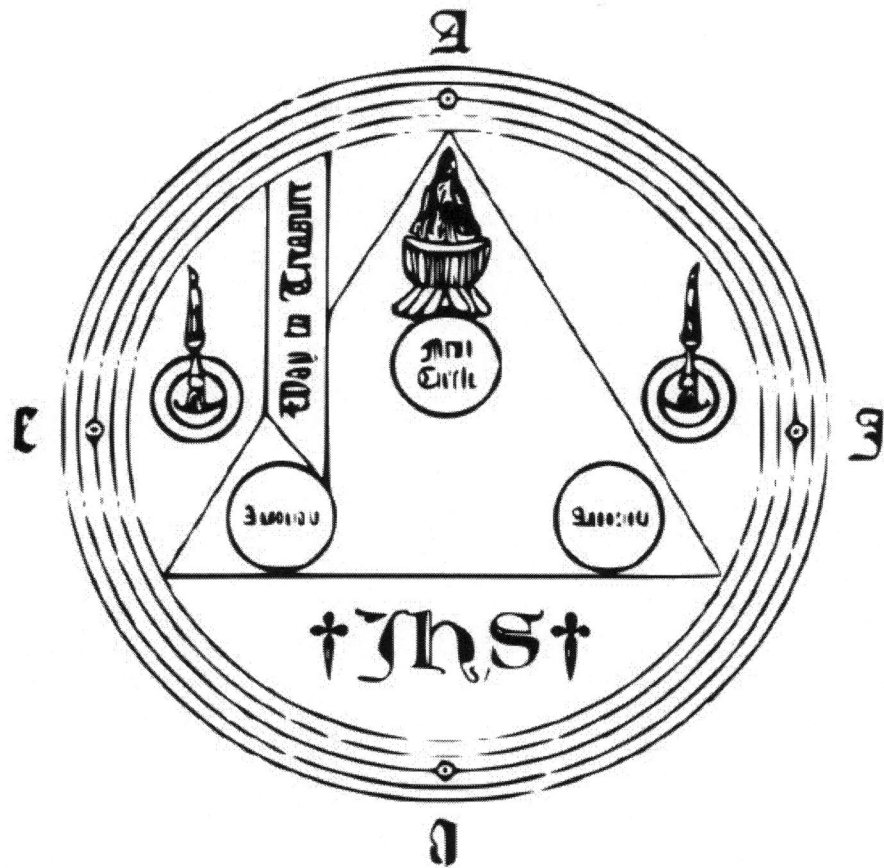

I:

Ubi quem volueris spiritum, hujus nomen et officium supra cognosces: imprimis autem ab omni pollutione minimum tres vel quatuor dies mundus esto in prima citatione, sic et spiritus postea obsequentiores erunt; fac et circulum, et voca spiritum, cum multa intentione primum vere anulum in manu contiietur: inde banc resitata benedictionem tuo nomine e socii, si praesto fuerit et effectum tui instituti sortieris, nec detrimentum e spiritibus senties imo tuae animae perditionem.

II:

In nomine domini nostri Jesus Christi, patris et filii et spiritus sancti: sancta Trinitas et inseparabilis unitas te invoco, ut sis mihi salus et defensio et protectio corporis et animae meae et omnium rerum mearum. Per virtutem sanctae crucis et per virtutem passionis tuae deprecor te Domine Jesus Christi, per merita beatissimae Mariae Virgini et matris tuae atque ominus sanctorum tuorum, ut mihi concedas gratiam et potestatem divinam super omnes malignos spiritus, ut quoscumque nominibus invocavero, statim ex omni parte conveniant, et voluntatem meam perfecte adimpleant qued mihi nihil nocentes, neque timorem inferentes, sed potens obedientes et ministrantes, tua distincte virtute praecipiente, mandata mea perficiant. Amen.

Sanctus, sanctus, dominus Deus sabaot, qui venturus est judicare vivos et mortuos: tu qui es primus et novissimus, rex regum et dominum dominantium Joth, Agladabrach, Elabiel, anarchi enatiel amaz in sedomel gayes tol ma elias ischiro atgadatasy mas heli messias per hac tua sancta nomina, et per omnia alia invocare et obsecro te Domine Jesu Christe, per quam nativitatem per baptismum tuum, per passionem et crucem tuam, per ascensionem tuam per adventum Spiritus Sancti paraclite per amaritudinae anime tuae quando exivi de corpore tuo per quinque vulnera tua, per sanguinem et aquam quae exierant de corpore tuo, per virtutem tuam, per sacramentum quod dedisti descipuit tui pridie quam passus fuisti per sanctam Trinitatem, per individuam anitatem, per beatam Mariam, matrem tuam, per Angelos, et arcangelos, per prophetas et patriarchas, et per omnes sancto tuos et per omnia sacramenta quae fiant in honore tuo; adoro et te obsecro, te benedicto tibi, et rogo ut acceptes orationes has et conjurationes et verba oris mei; quibus uti volucro peto Domine Jesu Christe: da mihi virtutem et potestatem tuam super omnes angelos tuos, qui de coelo ejecti sunt ad decipiendum genus humanum; ad attrahendum eos, ad constringendum, ad ligandum eos pariter et solvendum; et ad

THE GRAND GRIMOIRE

congregantum eos coram me; quae possunt, faciant et verba mea vocem que meam nullo modo contemnant, sed mihi et dictis meis obediant, et me tineant per humanitatem et misericaridam et gratiam tuam deprecor et peto et ADONAY amay hora videgora mitay hel suranay syota y fiesy, et per omnia uomina tua sancta per omnes sanctos et sanctos tuos, per angelos et archangelos, potestates, dominitiones et virtutes, et per illud nomen per quod Salomo costringebat daemone et conclusit ipso. Eth roceban hrangle goth joih athio venoh aubru et per omnium tua nomina quae scripta sunt in hoc librum et per virtutem sorundem, quatenus me potentem faciat con gregare contringere omnes tuos spiritus de coelo depulsos ut mihi veraciter de omnibus meis interrogatis de quibus quaram responsionem veracem tribuant et omnibus meis mandatis illi satis faciant sine laesione corporis et animae meae, et omnibus ad me pertinentium, per dominum nostrum Jesum Christum filium tuum, qui tecum vivit et tegnat in unitate spiritus sancti Deus, per omnia saecula.

III:

O pater omnipotens!, o filii sapiens, o spiritus sante corda hominum illustrans! vos tres in personis una vero deitas in substantia qui Adam et Evae in peccatis eorum perpercistis et propter eorum peccata mortem subjesti tu filii turpissima in lignoque sancte crucis sustinuisti. O misericordissime quando ad tuam confugio misericordiam, et supplico modis omnibus quibus possum per haec nomina sancta tui filii scilicet A et a et per omnia alia sua nomina, quatenus concedas mihi virtutem et potestatem tual, ut valeam tuos spiritusqui de coelo ejecti sunt, ante me citare, et ut ipsi mecum loquantur, et mandata mea perficiant statim et fine mora cum eorum voluntate, sine omni laesione corporis animae et honorum meorum. Amen.

IV:

O summa et eterna virtus altissimi! que te disponente his judicio vocatis vaycheon stimulamaton esphares tetagrammaton ilioram rion esytio existioneriona onera brasym moyn messias sodxer, EMMANUEL, SABAOTH, ADONAY, te adoro, te invoco, totius mentis viribus meis, imploro, quaenus per te praesentes orationes et consecrationes consequentur videlicet, et ubicumque maligni spiritus in virtute tuorum dominum sunt vocati, et voluntatem mei exorcisatores diligenter adimpleant fiat, fiat, fiat. Amen.

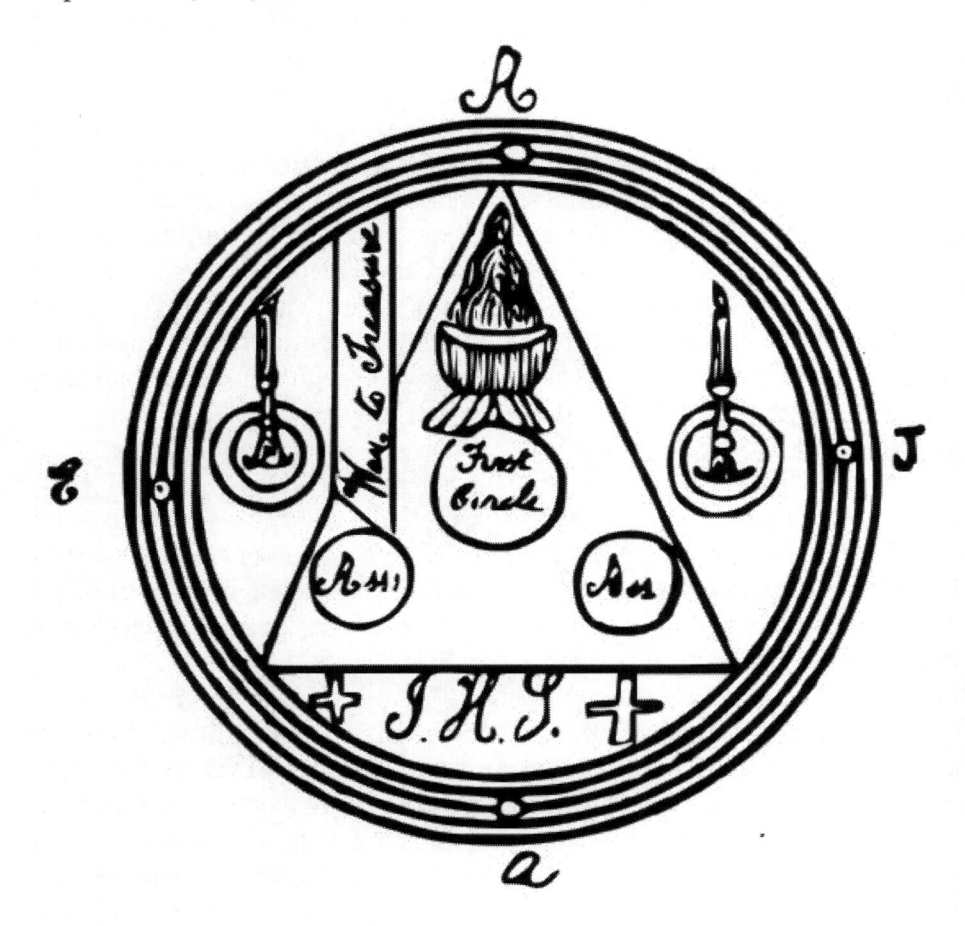

The Magick Secret or the Art of Speaking with the Dead:

For this operation it is necessary to attend midnight mass at Christmas and at midnight precisely to have a conversation with the inhabitants of the other world and at the moment that the priest lifts the host, bow down and with a frank and severe voice say "Esurgent mortuit et ac me veniut." As soon as you have pronounced these six words it is necessary to go to the cemetery and at the first tomb that meets your eye offer this prayer:

"Infernal powers, you who bring the turbid in the universe, abandon your obscure dwelling and retire to the other side of the River Styx."

Then remain there for a moment of silence. "If you have your power, he or she that interests me, I supplicate you in the name of the King of Kings to make him appear before me at the hour and moment that I will indicate to you."

After this ceremony, which is indispensable to carry out, take a fistful of earth and spread it as one sows grain in a field, saying in a low voice: "He who is in dust awake from his tomb and leave his ashes and answer the questions that I pose him in the name of the Father of all men."

Then bend a knee to the ground, turning your eyes to the East and when you see that the doors of the Sun are going to open, arm yourself with the two bones of the dead man that you will put in a cross of Saint Andrew. Then throw them at the first temple or church that offers itself to your eyes.

Having well-executed the aforesaid, set out in a western direction and when you have taken 5,900 steps, lay yourself down to sleep on the ground in an elongated position, holding the palms of your hand against your thighs, and your eyes to the sky towards the Moon and in this position, call he or she whom you wish to see, when you see the specter appear, solicit their presence with the following words "Ego sum te peto, et videre queo."

After these words, your eyes will be satisfied to see the object that dearest to you and give you the most pleasurable delight.

When you have obtained from the shadow which you have invoked, that which you believe to be to your satisfaction, send it away in this manner: "Return to the kingdom of the elect, I am content with you and your presence."

Then picking yourself up, return to the same tomb where you made the first prayer above which you need to make a cross with the end of your blade which you will be holding in your left hand.

The reader should not neglect any of the prescribed ceremonies otherwise he could incur some risk.

Secrets of the Magick Art:

Observe that these secrets can not be employed by those who have not done all that is described in Sections II, III and IV of the first book of this volume.

The Composition of Death, or Philosopher's Stone:

Take a new earthen pot, put in it a pound of red copper with half a bottle of nitric acid. Boil it for half an hour. Afterward, add three ounces of verdegris (copper carbonate), and boil for one hour. Then add two and a half ounces of arsenic, and boil one hour. Add three ounces of oak bark, well pulverized, and let it boil a half hour, add a 64 fluid ounces of rose water boil twelve minutes, then add three ounces of lampblack, and let it boil until the composition is good. To see whether it is cooked enough, dip a nail in it; if it adheres, remove it. It will produce a pound and a half of good gold. If it does not adhere, it is proof that it has not cooked enough; the liquor can serve four times.

To Make the Divining Rod and Make it Work:

At the moment the sun appears on the horizon, take your left hand a virgin branch from the wild hazel tree, and cut it in three strokes while saying: "I collect you in the name of ELOHIM, MITRATHON, ADONAY and SEMIPHORAS, so that you have the virtue of the rod of Moses and Jacob, to discover all that I will want to know. To make it work, hold it tightly in your hands by the two ends which make the fork, and say: I command you in the name of ELOHIM, MITRATHON, ADONAY and

THE GRAND GRIMOIRE

SEMIPHORAS to reveal to me, etc."

To Enchant Firearms:

Say: "God has a share in it and the devil has the exit", and when you fire, say the following while crossing your left leg over your right: "non tradas Dominum nostrum Jesum Christum. Mathon. Amen."

To Win Any Time one Plays the Lottery:

Lying down, recite three times the following prayer, after what to you will put it under your pillow, written on virgin parchment, on which you will have a mass of the Holy Spirit said, and during sleep the genius of your planet will come and tell you the hour that you must get your ticket.

"Domine Jesu Christe, qui dixisti ego sum via, veritas et vita, ecce enim veritatem dilexisti, incerta et occulta sapientiæ tuæ manifestasti mihi, adhuc quæ reveles in hac nocte sicut ita revelatum fuit parvulis solis, incognita et ventura unaque alia me doceas, ut possim omnia cognoscere, si et si sit; ita monstra mihi montem ornatum omni nivo bono, pulchrum et gratum pomarium, aut quandam rem gratam, sin autem ministra mihi ignem ardentem, vel aquarum currentem vel aliam quamcumque rem quæ Domino placeat, et vel Angeli ARIEL, Rubiel et Barachiel sitis mihi multúm amatores et factores ad opus istud obtinendum quod cupio scire, videre cognoscere et prævidere per illum Deum qui venturus est judicare vivos et mortuos, et sæculum per ignem. Amen."

Say three "Our Fathers" and three "Hail Mary's" for the souls left in purgatory.

To speak with the Spirits on the Eve of St. John the Baptist:

From eleven at night until Midnight go stand by a fern, and say: "I ask of God that the spirits with which I wish to speak will appear at precisely midnight"; and at three-quarters repeat nine times these five words: "Bar, Kirabar, Alli, Alla Tetragrammaton."

To be Insensible to Torture:

Write these lines on a small piece of paper, which you will then swallow.

Dismas et gestas damnatur potestas.
Disma et gestas damnatur.
Ad astra levatur.

When you will have to be tortured say: "This rope is so soothing to the my limbs, like the Holy Virgin's milk to Our Lord."

To Compel one to Dance Completely Naked:

On Eve of St. John the Baptist, gather at midnight, three walnut leaves, three sweet marjoram plants, three myrtle plants, and three vervain plants. Dry it all in the shade, and make it into a powder. When you want to make use of the powder, throw some like a small pinch of tobacco into the air of the room where there are the people whom you wish to enjoy.

To Make oneself Invisible:

Take a black cat, and a new pot, a mirror, a lighter, coal and tinder. Gather water from a fountain at the strike of midnight.

After you light your fire, and put the cat in the pot. Hold the cover with your left hand without moving nor looking behind you, no matter what noises you may hear.

After having made it boil 24 hours, put the boiled cat on a new dish. Take the meat and throw it over your left shoulder, saying these words: "accipe quod tibi do, et nihil ampliùs."

Then put the bones one by one under the teeth on the left side, while looking at yourself in the mirror; and if they are do not work, throw them away, repeating the same words each time until you find the right bone; and as soon you cannot see yourself any more in the mirror, withdraw, moving backwards, while saying: "Pater, in manus tuas commendo spiritum meum." This bone you must keep.

To Render Oneself Favorable to Judges:

Upon seeing the Judge, say these words: "Phalay, Phalay, Phalay; preside in my favor, let your power shine. Make me satisfied."

To be Impervious to White Arms:

With the head of a needle, write these words on your arm: "Ales C Dales C Tolas C." Then put the needle in the middle cross, from which no blood will flow.

To Make the Garter of Twenty Miles per Hour:

Buy a young wolf under one year old, and cut its throat with a new knife, in the hour of Mars, pronouncing these words: "Adhumatis cados ambulavit in fortitudine cibi ilius;" then cut his skin into broad garters of an inch, and write there upon the same words that you said while slaughtering it. Write the first letter with your blood, the second with that of the wolf, and continue in the same way until the end of the sentence.

After it is written and dries, it is necessary to cover it by wrapping the garter in white cloth, and to attach two purple ribbons to the two ends, so to tie the garters to the knee braces; Make sure that no woman or girl sees the garters; also remove the garters before crossing a river, Less it loses it's power.

Formula for a Plaster to Travel Ten Miles per Hour:

Take two ounces of human fat, one ounce of oil of stag, one ounce of oil of bay-tree, one ounce of fat of stag, one ounce of natural mummy, a half-cup of spirit of wine, and seven Verbena leaves. Boil the whole in a new pot, until half-reduction, then form a plàster of it on a fresh wolf skin.

When you wear it on the spleen, you go like the wind. To not fall when you are done, take three drops of blood in a glass of white wine and soak your feet in the wine.

Composition of the Ink for Writing Pacts:

The pacts should not be written with ordinary ink. It must be changed each time that there is occasion to write a pact, that is to say, whenever the appellation of a spirit is made. Place river-water in a new, water-proof earthenware pot, together with the powder described below. Take sprigs of fern gathered on the Eve of St. John and vine twigs cut in the full moon of March. Kindle this wood by means of virgin paper, and when the water boils the ink will be made. It must be changed each time that there is occasion to write, that is to say, whensoever the appellation of a spirit is undertaken.

    10 oz. Of Gall nuts
    3 oz. Of Roman Vitriol or Green Copper
    3 oz. Of Rock Alum or dried Gum Arabic.

Make a fine powder, and when you would compose the ink, use as described above.

Solomon's Mirror:

How to Make Solomon's Mirror (in nomine domini. amen.)

The manner upon which the Kabbalist Scholars relied to make the Mirror of Solomon, David's son, who had the gift of wisdom and the occult science; this mirror is made in forty-eight days, starting from the new moon until the following full one. You will see (in this mirror) all of the hidden things that you desire in the name of our Lord.

First, abstain from any carnal action or thought for the entire aforementioned time and meanwhile do many pious and compassionate deeds.

Take a shiny and well cleaned plate of steel and write in the four corners these precise words in the blood of a White Dove: JEHOVA, ELOHIM, MITRATHON, ADONAY. Then put the steel plate in a piece of new white cloth and when you observe the New Moon one hour after the sun has set go to the window and gazing at the sky and the moon say with devotion: "O rex eternæ Deus! Creator ineffabilis, qui cuncta as hominis sanitatem meagratio, et occulto judicio creasti respice me (N.N.), indignissimum servum tuum, et ad intentionem meam, et mittere mihi dignare angelum Anael, in speculum istud, qui mandet, et inspiret et jubeat cum sociis suis, et subditis nostris ut in nominee tuo qui fuisti, es et eris potens, et jus, jud, judicent mihi quecumque ab illis exposcam."

THE GRAND GRIMOIRE

Take some ashes made from Laurel wood and add some perfume into it in three shots saying: "In hoc, per hoc, et cum hoc, quod effundo ante conspectum tuum, Deus meus, trinus et unus benedictus et per excelsus qui vides super Cherubin et Seraphin et venturus est judicare seculum per ignem."

Recite this prayer three times, blow on the mirror and then call out this invocation: "Veni Anael, et tibi complaceat esse per socios tuos mecum, in nomine patris potentissimi, in nomine filio sapientissimo, in nomine spiritus amabilissimi. Veni Anael, in nomini terribilis JEHOVA; veni Anael in virtute immortalis Eliom; veni Anael in brachio omnipotentis Mitraton; veni Anael in potentia sacratissimi ADONAY; veni ad me (N.N.) in ispeculo isto, et jubeat subditis tuis ut cum amore gaudio et pace ostendat mihi occulta in oculis meis. Amen."

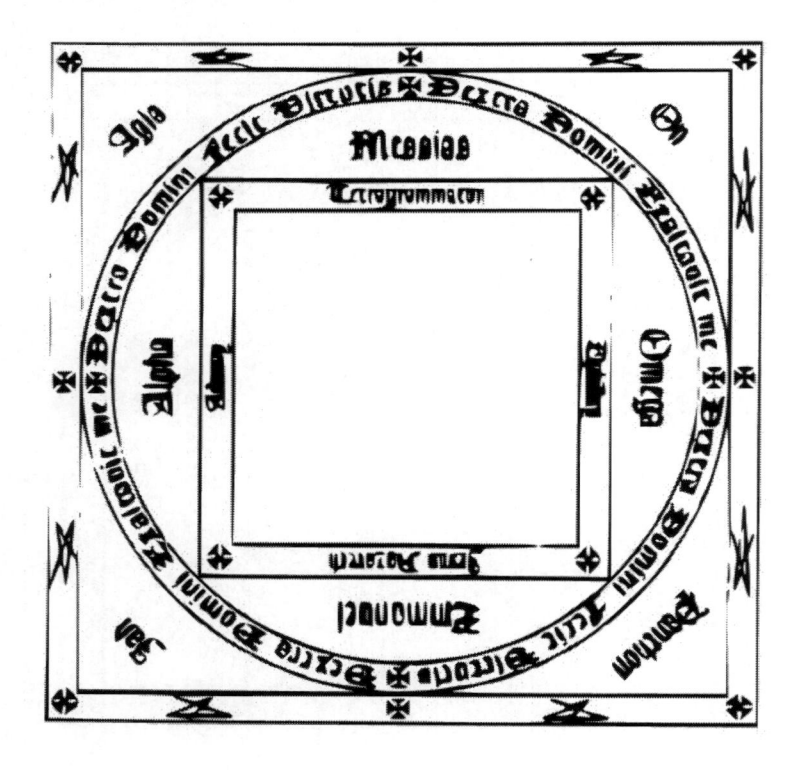

This said, raise your eyes to the sky and say: "Domini Deus

omnipotens, cujus nutu omnia moventur, exaudi deprecationem meum et desiderium meum tibi complaceat, respice domini speculum istud, et benedice illi ut Anael, unus ex subditis fuisse sistat in illo cum sociis et satisfaciat mihi famulo tuo (N.N.), cui vivis et regnas benedictus et excelsus, in saecula saeculorum. Amen."

After the aforementioned prayer, cross yourself and the mirror, and this you will do everyday for as long as it takes to make the mirror. In the end, the angel Anael will appear in the guise of a most handsome young man will greet you and command his companions to obey you. Be aware that 48 days are not always necessary to obtain what you intend; often he appears after 14 days, that depends on the intention and devotion of the Operator.

So when the spirit appears to you, as him everything that you wish and request that he appear to you whenever you call him to satisfy your requests. Then you will see everything you wish to see without reciting the preceding oration; but having anointed him with scent (the scent of Anael is Saffron) say the following:

Oration:

"Veni Anael, veni tibi complaceat esse per socios tuos mecum, in nomini mecum, in nomini Patris potentissimi, in nomini Filii sapientissimi, in nomine Spiritus Sancti amabilissimi; veni Anael, in virtutis immortalis ELOHIM; veni Anael, in brachio omnipotentis Mitraton; veni Anael, in potentia sacratissimi ADONAY; veni ad me (N.N.) in speculo isto, et jubeas subditis tuis, ut cum amore, gaudio et pace ostendam mihi occulta inoculis meis. Amen, Amen."

After you have recited this oration he will appear to you and satisfy all of your desires.

Method of taking Leave of the angel Anael:

"Gratias tibi ago Anael quod venisti, et petitioni meæ satisfecisti, ibi in pace et placeat tibi redire quando to vocavero."

THE GRAND GRIMOIRE

Cross yourself and the mirror.

Table of Auspicious and Inauspicious Days:

Auspicious Days	Month	Inauspicious Days
2, 10, 27 and 31	January	13 and 23
7, 8 and 18	February	2, 10, 17 and 22
3, 9, 14 and 16	March	13, 19, 23 and 28
5 and 17	April	18, 20, 29 and 30
1, 2, 4, 6, 9 and 15	May	10, 17 and 20
3, 5, 7, 9, 12 and 23	June	4 and 20
2, 6, 10, 23 and 30	July	5, 13 and 27
5, 7, 10, 14 and 29	August	2, 13, 27 and 31
6, 10, 13, 18 and 30	September	13, 16, 18 and 19
13, 16, 25 and 31	October	3, 9 and 27
1, 13, 23 and 30	November	6 and 25
10, 20 and 29	December	15, 26 and 31

Observation:

Many wise men believe this table was dictated to Abraham by an angel and that it determined his actions: he neither sowed nor transplanted except on auspicious days and for this reason everything went marvelously for him. If your plowmen did likewise their yield would certainly increase.

The Secret of the Black Hen:

The famous secret of the Black Hen, a secret without which one can not count on the success of any Kabbala, was lost for a long time: after much investigation we have succeeded in finding it and the tests which we have carried out, to assure ourselves that it was positively that which we sought, exactly matched our expectations. Therefore we are completely satisfied. It is to share our happiness with all those who have the courage to imitate us that we have transcribed it.

THE GRAND GRIMOIRE

Take a Black Hen that has never been laid eggs and that has never been approached by a rooster and in taking her make certain that she does not cry out so that you will have to do this at eleven at night, when she is sleeping. Take her neck and close her throat so that she can not scream.

Then go where two streets form a cross and at midnight precisely make a circle with a cyprus branch, go into the middle of the circle and cut the hen' body into two parts uttering the following words three times: ELOHIM, ESSAIM, search and then turn your gaze toward the East, kneel and recite the prayer:

Prayer to the Omnipotent in Thanksgiving:

"Omnipotent God, heavenly father, who created all things for the service and use of man, I humbly thank you, that in your great goodness and that you have permitted that I could make a pact with a spirit that is a rebel of your authority and subdue it to obey me in fulfilling all of my needs. I thank you, O omnipotent God, for the good that you have done me tonight to have shown myself to be worthy to have granted to me, miserable creature, your precious favors and to present, great God, now that I have come to know the force and power of your great promises, when you said: "seek and you shall find", "knock and the door shall be opened" as you have recommended to raise the poor, condescend O great God to inspire me to true sentiment of charity so that I can spread with this Great Work a great portion of the possessions your great divinity permitted that I could receive. Let it be, O great God, that I can enjoy these great riches that I possess, with tranquility and do not permit any rebel spirit to harm my enjoyment of these precious treasures over which you permit me to own. Inspire in me, O great God, the necessary sentiment to unbind me from the grips of the devil and all maleficent spirits. I trust, O great God, in the Father, the Son, and the Holy Spirit and in your saintly protection. Amen."

Oration to Protect Oneself from Evil Spirits:

"O omnipotent Father, O Mother, the most tender of all mothers, O admirable example of the sentiments, O Son, O flower of all sons, soul, spirit, harmony and number of all orders, preserve us, protect us, guide us and be propitious. Amen."

Great Invocation to Summon the Spirit with whom one wishes to the pact excerpted from The Great Clavicle:

"Emperor LUCIFER, master of all the rebel spirits, I ask you to be favorable in my summons of your Great Minister LUCIFUGE ROFOCALE, since I wish to make a pact with him. I also request that you, Prince BELZEBUTH, protect me in my undertaking; O Come ASTAROTH BE propitious and ensure that the great LUCIFUGE appears to me tonight in human guise and without emitting foul odors and he grant me as per the pact that I will present to him, all of the riches which I require. O great LUCIFUGE, I request that you abandon your dwelling, in whatever part of the world it should be, to come and speak with me. Otherwise, I will force you by the power of the great living God and his dear Son and the Holy Spirit: obey now, or I will eternally torment you by the authority of the powerful words of Solomon's great Clavicle of which he made use to oblige the rebel Spirits to receive his pact; therefore, appear as quickly as possible or I will continually torment you by the authority of the powerful words of the Clavicle:

Aglon, Tetragram, vaycheon stimulamaton ezphares Tetragrammaton, olyaram irion esytion existion eryona onera orasim mozm messias soter Emanuel Sabaoth ADONAY, te adoro et te invoco. Amen."

At that moment the foul spirit will appear, dressed in a scarlet outfit with braids, a yellow shirt, green pants, his head resembles that of a dog, but he has the ears of an ass, with two horns, legs and feet like a heifer. He will ask you your demands; you give them as you think best since he will not be able to disobey you and he can make you one of the richest and therefore happiest of men.

Before you do what has been explained you need to make your devotions. Say your prayers and be above reproach; this is so essential that in doing the opposite you could end up at the spirits command, instead of him being at yours.

Other Magick Secrets:

To prevent a Woman from Conceiving:

To prevent a woman, with whom you are having relations, from having children, take a sponge the size of a nutmeg, and soak it with pure milk mixed with a little fine oil. Put it in her left hand and walk away from her and every time you do this you will be sure to gave good results.

To Find Out whether a Woman can Have Children:

Take the fat of a deer, melt it in hot water; the woman should drink it on an empty stomach and afterward take a hot bath. If this gives her pain in her stomach, then she will have children, otherwise not.

To Make Three Young Ladies, or rather Three Spirits come into your Room after Dinner:

Preparation:

Eat neither meat nor fatty foods for three days; on the fourth day clean your room as soon as you have arisen from bed, fast for the entire day and ensure that no one enters the room all day and that there is nothing hung on the walls, neither clothes, nor hats, nor bird cages, nor curtains on the windows or on the bed and above all, put freshly washed white linens on the bed.

Ceremony:

After dinner, go secretly to the room that you have prepared, light a good fire, put a clean white cloth on the table and three chairs around the table and three loaves of bread and three glasses of clear, fresh water at each place. Then put a recliner or chair beside your bed and get into bed.

Upon entering the room the three persons will seat themselves beside the fire and taking refreshment and thank he or she who has received them, since, if he is a man who makes the ceremony three ladies will come, and if it is a woman, three men will come. The three spirits will choose by lots among themselves to determine who will remain seated in the chair beside your bed to converse with you until midnight.

At midnight she will leave with her companions without you having to ask her to leave, as for the other two, they will remain by the fire while the other converses with you beside your bed and you will to ask her about any art or science that you desire and she will immediately answer your questions, you can ask her the location of the nearest hidden treasure and she will reveal to you the most opportune time and place to recover it. She will also be there accompanied by her two companions to protect you from any infernal spirit who could be in possession of the treasure. When she leaves, she will give you a ring which will make you lucky in any game when you wear it and if you place it on a young maid's finger you can make her your wife.

Note: Leave the window open so that they may enter and you can repeat this operation and make them come as many times as you wish. You should repeat the following prayer after each conjuration:

"O summa et eterna virtus altissimi! que te disponente his judicio vocatis vaycheon stimulamaton esphares tetagrammaton ilioram rion esytio existioneriona onera brasym moyn messias sodxer, EMMANUEL, SABAOTH, ADONAY, te adoro, te invoco, totius mentis viribus meis, imploro, quaenus per te praesentes orationes et consecrationes consequentur videlicet, et ubicumque maligni spiritus in virtute tuorum dominum sunt vocati, et voluntatem mei exorcisatores diligenter adimpleant fiat, fiat, fiat. Amen."

To be Lucky in Every Enterprise:

THE GRAND GRIMOIRE

Take a green frog, cut off its head and his four feet. Then on a Friday with a full Moon put them in an elder tree and keep them there for twenty-one days, removing them on the twenty-first day precisely at midnight.

Then expose the parts of the frog to the light of the Moon for three nights. Afterward, dry the frog parts in a new earthernware pot that has never been used. Take the dried frog parts, and grind to a powder. Mix the powder in equal measure with earth taken from a cemetery, if possible from the grave of someone in your family.

Carry the powder mixture with you, it will help you succeed in any undertaking.

To Make a Woman Disclose her Secrets:

Take the heart of a pigeon and the head of a frog. Dry them as above, and reduce them to fine powder. Put the powder into a little purse, and add moss for fragrance.

Put the purse under the woman's ear while she is sleeping, fifteen minutes later, she will unveil all of her secrets. Make certain to remove the purse a few minutes after she has stopped speaking otherwise she could fall into delirium.

To see and do the Supernatural:

Put a gold studded plate under your tongue, it should be half the size of your thumb. Under your feet put the border of a mortuary sheet or linen and hold a quince tree branch in your hand. Abstain from having sexual relations for thirty-five days, for thirty-five is the number that puts you under the protection of favorable constellations and sorcery and with this secret one can do prodigious deeds, as did Moses with this secret did supernatural things.

To make Everything in an Apartment Appear Black:

Soak the wick of the lamp used to light the apartment in well beaten sea foam, adding to the lamp oil some sulfur and lead oxide in equal parts, and all those who enter the room will appear drunk and delirious.

Glue to attach Crystals:

Take some wine spirits and whitest and clearest Gum Arabic. Liquefy the Gum Arabic with the spirits. Heat up the two broken pieces in the fire, then with a little brush apply the glue to the two pieces. Attach the two pieces, and hold together until they have cooled.

Glue to Repair Porcelain Vases:

Take two fresh egg whites, mix them together, add a little quicklime. Put a little of this mixture on the broken pieces, hold them together for two or three minutes. Then boil them with milk and the cracks will become invisible.

The Secrets of Love:

Of Reciprocal Love between a Man and a Woman.

There is nothing more natural to man than loving and being loved. Without invoking Venus or Cupid, who are the dominant divinities regarding this noble passion of man, every day produces material substances that are favorable to success in love. One often finds on the forehead of a newborn foal, a little piece of flesh that has marvelous virtue in love. Dry it in a new pot, and wear it, especially on Fridays, since this is the day dedicated to Venus, Goddess of Love.

Another Love Secret:

Take a gold ring that is studded with a small diamond that has not been worn by anyone. Wrap it in a piece of green fabric and for nine days and nine nights wear it against your skin over your heart. On the ninth day, before the Sun rises, engrave the following word inside the ring: Scheva, with a new scribe or engraver.

Find a way to have three hairs of the person who you want to love you, unite them with three of your own hairs, while saying: "Body, that you could love me, that your desires could be as passionate as mine, by Scheva's most potent virtue." Tie the hairs in a love snare knot around the ring. Wrap the ring in a piece of silk, and wear it against your skin over your heart for another six days. On the seventh day, Fast. On an empty stomach, unwrap the ring and give it to the person you desire to love you.

If your ring is accepted then you can be certain to be loved by that person. If the ring is refused, rest assured that the heart of that person belongs to another and in that case, you should seek your fortune elsewhere.

Other Secrets that Achieve the Same Effect:

Here is the secret that the wise Kabbalists have called "Apple of Love" which is prepared as follows:

Go pick an apple from a tree on a Friday morning before sunrise. Write your name with your blood on a piece of paper and also write the name of the person whom you wish to love you. On another sheet of paper, write the name Scheva, also in your own blood.

Find a means of procuring three strands of that person's hair, which you will unite with three of yours. Cut the apple in half, and remove the seeds. In the place of the seeds, place the pieces of paper. Take the apple and tie it back together, with the united hairs, using a green myrtle twig to twist together the two halves of the apple like a tourniquet.

Dry well in the oven, and wrap them in bay and myrtle leaves. Have a well trusted person put the apple under the young woman's pillow without her noticing. In a few days you will notice the appearance of her love.

THE GRAND GRIMOIRE

Popular Beliefs:

There are individuals who believe in bad omens as well as good omens. They perceive the following as bad omens:

-If the first person they meet in the morning is a monk or priest.
-Hearing the cry of an owl or a bat at night, or when a cat meows.
-Tipping over a salt shaker with salt spilled on the table.
-Putting one's shirt inside-out when one rises in the morning.
-Meeting on an empty stomach.
-Meeting a hare or a black goat, a snake or a boar on an empty stomach.
-Hearing a hen sing.
-Putting one's right shoe on first.
-On having a nose bleed, seeing only three drops come from the right nostril.
-Upon going out, hitting something with one's feet.
-Putting knives in the shape of a cross on the table.
-When a deceased person has one leg shorter than the other or open eyes, then another person will die in that house by the years' end.
-When there is ringing in your right ear it means your enemies are speaking ill of you. When the left ear rings it is your friends speaking of you.

They take the following instead to be good omens:

-Meeting, as the first person you see in the morning, a baker with bread or a concubine.
-The hunter will be fortunate in the hunt if the first person he meets merits contempt.
-Seeing a spider weaving it's web in the morning is a good omen.

-If the fire gives off sparks of joy.
-If, when the dog is sleeping, it points its nose to the door, then you will have a visitor.
-To find out whether someone who is ill will die of his illness, put a little salt in his hand and if it liquefies, that is a bad sign.

THE GRAND GRIMOIRE

-In uniting the first and last names of a married couple, the one who has odd letters will die first.

-In leaving the house, if someone asks where you are going, return home quickly for fear that some misfortune might befall you.

-There are people who attempt to justify this erroneous belief, allotting that Judith is leaving Betulia to go meet Holocerne, beseeching the priest to not ask her where she is going for fear that in the questioning she would be obligated to renounce the undertaking.

THE GRAND GRIMOIRE

Made in the USA
San Bernardino, CA
08 February 2020